RIVERS

RIVERS

FROM MOUNTAIN STREAMS TO CITY RIVERBANKS

CLAUDIA MARTIN

amber
BOOKS

Published by Amber Books Ltd
United House
North Road
London N7 9DP
United Kingdom
www.amberbooks.co.uk
Instagram: amberbooksltd
Facebook: amberbooks
Twitter: @amberbooks
Pinterest: amberbooksltd

ISBN: 978-1-83886-102-5

Project Editor: Michael Spilling
Designer: Keren Harragan
Picture Research: Justin Willsdon

Printed in China

Contents

Introduction

Rivers cover just a fraction of a per cent of the world's land, yet they are of immeasurable importance to humans and the countless other species that depend on freshwater for life and growth. It is hard to think of a major city that does not lie on a river or other major water source. Early settlements grew up beside rivers, relying on them for drinking water, fishing, washing and disposing of waste. Over the centuries, humans learned to build boats for transport and trade. We constructed ingenious irrigation canals and hydropower devices. Rivers were used for defence and for demarcating borders, resulting in desperate battles being fought on and beside rivers, from the 1690 Battle of the Boyne between warring kings, to the 1945 battle of Remagen for control of the Ludendorff Bridge over the Rhine. Today, battles are still fought over rivers, from wars of words over dam-building between conservationists and governments, to struggles between those suffering from water insecurity in the world's increasingly drought-stricken regions.

ABOVE:
Li River, China
The Li River winds its way between the karst formations of Guilin.

OPPOSITE:
Columbia River, Canada
Seen from above, the river's braided channel builds slowly evolving patterns.

North America

The longest river in North America is the Missouri, which flows for 3767km (2341 miles) from Montana's Rocky Mountains to its confluence with the Mississippi at St Louis. When measured in combination with its tributaries and the mighty Mississippi, the Missouri river system is the fourth longest in the world, after the Nile, Amazon and Yangtze. The Missouri drainage basin covers one-quarter of all the agricultural land in the United States. However, as with all North America's rivers, the Missouri's importance stretches beyond irrigation, through history and the march of progress. Before European colonization of the region, countless Native American peoples depended on the river for fish and transport. The river played a starring role in the expansion of the United States, as the major trails to the west, such as the Oregon and Santa Fe, began at the Missouri. During the 19th and 20th centuries, 15 dams were built on the river's main stretch. Through the same period, the river's waters were polluted by industry and agriculture along its banks. Channel control reduced the sediment carried downstream, destroying vital habitat for fish, amphibians and birds. Yet, today, portions of the river and its surrounding habitats are protected as national monuments, wildlife refuges and a National Wild and Scenic Rivers System. The Missouri's story is not unique: across North America, the same cooperation and destruction, advance and retreat, can be seen in the stories of every river, from the St Lawrence to the Rio Grande.

OPPOSITE:
Kenai River, Alaska, USA
Every year, the Kenai experiences two runs each of sockeye, coho and king salmon, when the fish swim upriver – past waiting bears and anglers – to reach the spawning ground that was their birthplace. After spawning, the adult fish die, while the grounds become nurseries for eggs and growing juveniles.

Kenai River, Alaska, USA
Before the arrival of European settlers, the Kenai River region was one of the most densely populated in Alaska. It was home to the Dena'ina people, who called the river Kahtnu. The river's seasonal wealth of salmon was turned into a year-round resource by drying the fish then burying them in well-insulated cold storage pits.

OPPOSITE:

Kluane National Park and Reserve, Canada
Numerous rivers and creeks wind their way across the tundra from the high glaciers of Kluane National Park. Rafting on the Alsek River offers glimpses of the park's populations of black and grizzly bears as they search for bearberries, crowberries, horsetail and sedge in the river valley.

RIGHT:

Yukon River, Canada
The Yukon River flows for 3190km (1980 miles) from the Llewellyn Glacier, in British Colombia, to the Bering Sea. The river's name is probably a contraction of the Gwich'in phrase for 'white water river'.

E.L. Patton Yukon River Bridge, Alaska, USA
In all the Yukon's great length, there are just four road bridges spanning the waterway, including the E.L. Patton Yukon River Bridge, which supports both the Dalton Highway and the Alaska Pipeline. The pipeline carries oil for 1288km (800 miles) from the northern oilfields of Prudhoe Bay to the port of Valdez.

PREVIOUS PAGES:
**Three Sisters,
Bow River, Canada**
Reflecting the Three Sisters peaks, the Bow River flows near Canmore, Alberta. The Three Sisters take their name from a story told by the Îyârhe Nakoda about the trickster I-ktomni, who promised his three sisters in marriage whenever he wanted to get out of trouble.

FAR LEFT:
Bow River, Calgary, Canada
The Bow River flows through central Calgary, where its banks and bridges form the Bow River Pathway for pedestrians and cyclists. The river divides around numerous islands, including St Patrick's, home to one of the city's best-loved parks and a city centre nesting site for eagles, owls and songbirds.

LEFT:
**Morant's Curve,
Bow River, Canada**
On the Bow Valley Parkway between Banff and Lake Louise is the viewpoint of Morant's Curve. It was made famous by Nicholas Morant, the Canadian Pacific Railway's staff photographer from 1929 to 1935 and 1944 until 1981.

OPPOSITE:

Kicking Horse River, Yoho National Park, Canada
In Yoho National Park, the Kicking Horse surges through the narrow channel of Kicking Horse Canyon, wearing the rock into strange peaks and cauldrons. The river was named by Scottish geologist James Hector, a member of the 1857–60 Palliser Expedition, when he was kicked by his horse nearby.

RIGHT:

Wapta Falls, Kicking Horse River, Canada
Around 18m (59ft) high and 107m (351ft) wide, Wapta is the largest of the three waterfalls on the Kicking Horse River. The falls take their name from an Îyârhe Nakoda word for 'river'.

St Lawrence River, Montréal, Canada
The St Lawrence flows northeastward from Lake Ontario to the Gulf of St Lawrence, which at 226,000 sq km (87,000 sq miles) is one of the largest estuaries in the world. The city of Montréal lies on an island where the St Lawrence River meets the Ottawa River. The 1930 steel truss Jacques Cartier Bridge connects the island with the river's south bank.

St Lawrence River, Montréal, Canada
Each winter the St Lawrence freezes over. Icebreakers keep
the Port of Montréal open year round. However, ships are
occasionally stranded by ice jams, caused by heavy winds
breaking off ice sheets connected to the shore.

St Lawrence River, Canada
The St Lawrence churns as it surges past one of over 2000
islands. The largest archipelago is the Thousand Islands,
comprising 1864 islands scattered over 80km (50 miles) as the
river exits Lake Ontario.

ABOVE:

Belknap Bridge, McKenzie River, Oregon, USA
Opened in 1966, the current bridge is the fourth covered bridge on this site. Around 14,000 covered bridges were built in the United States, most in the 19th century. Today, between 800 and 1000 remain. Covered bridges are timber truss structures with a roof and siding that protect the wooden supports from weather and extend their life.

RIGHT:

Sahalie Falls, McKenzie River, Oregon, USA
In the Willamette National Forest, the McKenzie plunges over a 30m (100ft) natural dam that was formed around 3000 years ago by a thick lava flow from nearby Belknap Crater. In addition to such natural dams, the McKenzie River watershed also has six human-made dams, part of the Carmen–Smith Hydroelectric Project.

LEFT:

Columbia River, Astoria, Oregon, USA

Founded in 1811 where the Columbia River flows into the Pacific Ocean, the port city of Astoria was a vital post for US exploration of the West. Before reaching Astoria, the Columbia River has journeyed for 2000km (1243 miles) from Columbia Lake in British Columbia's Rocky Mountains.

RIGHT:

Multnomah Falls, Multnomah Creek, Oregon, USA

In the Columbia Gorge, Multnomah Creek falls 189m (620ft) in two steps. A legend told by the local Multnomah people explains that the waterfall was formed when, to save her village from the plague, a girl sacrificed herself to the Great Spirit by jumping off the cliff.

LEFT:
Blackfoot River, Montana, USA
Fed by snowmelt and springs of the Continental Divide, the Blackfoot flows westward to join the Clark Fork River, Montana's largest river by volume. The Blackfoot featured in Norman Maclean's semi-autobiographical 1976 novella about brothers growing up in Montana, *A River Runs Through It*.

RIGHT:
Blackfoot River, Montana, USA
The Blackfoot is clean, cold and deep, making it an ideal habitat for trout, including brown, rainbow, cutthroat and bull. The bull trout is classed as vulnerable because it requires water colder than 55°F (13°C) and low levels of silt, factors that are impacted by logging and construction.

FAR LEFT:

**Hudson River,
New York, USA**
Manhattan lies between the East River (lower left) and the Hudson River (lower right), which join in the Upper New York Bay. Despite its name, the East River is a saltwater tidal strait. After flowing through the Upper Bay, the Hudson passes under the Verrazzano Bridge at the Narrows, runs through the Lower Bay, then drains into the Atlantic.

LEFT TOP:

**Hudson River,
New York, USA**
A freighter loaded with asphalt journeys down the Hudson. The river is navigable by ocean-going vessels as far north as Albany, around 220km (135 miles) from New York City.

LEFT BOTTOM:

**Tarrytown Light,
Hudson River,
New York, USA**
Built in 1883, the Tarrytown Light warned ships away from the shoals off Sleepy Hollow, 48km (30 miles) north of New York City. The light was decommissioned in 1961 after General Motors reclaimed the dangerous stretch of river near the lighthouse to expand its Tarrytown Assembly Plant.

FAR LEFT:

Delaware River, Philadelphia, Pennsylvania, USA

The Benjamin Franklin Bridge links the city of Philadelphia with Camden, New Jersey. Completed in 1926, the steel suspension bridge is 2918m (9573ft) long. For the first three years of its life, the bridge's span was the world's longest, until the completion of the Ambassador Bridge between Detroit, Michigan, and Windsor, Ontario.

LEFT TOP:

Cumberland River, Kentucky, USA

The Cumberland River and its tributaries wind through Kentucky and Tennessee, cutting a series of gorges, waterfalls and arches in the sedimentary rock at Big South Fork. The river was named in 1758 by Virginian Thomas Walker, after England's Duke of Cumberland.

LEFT BOTTOM:

Kentucky River, Kentucky, USA

A tributary of the Ohio River, the Kentucky flows for 418km (260 miles) through Kentucky's Cumberland Mountains and Bluegrass region, named for its *Poa* grass, which has blue seed heads.

LEFT:

Mississippi River, Minnesota, USA

Minneapolis cloaks both banks of the Mississippi, around 290km (180 miles) south of the river's source in Lake Itasca. The St Anthony Falls Lock and Dam (pictured) were built in central Minneapolis to allow commercial navigation of the upper stretches of the river, but the lock was closed in 2015 to prevent the spread of invasive Asian carp.

RIGHT:

Mississippi River, Louisiana, USA

Tankers transport oil to the refineries and petrochemical plants along the Mississippi River north of New Orleans. Louisiana's fortunes have been closely linked with the extraction and processing of fossil fuels since the mid-20th century.

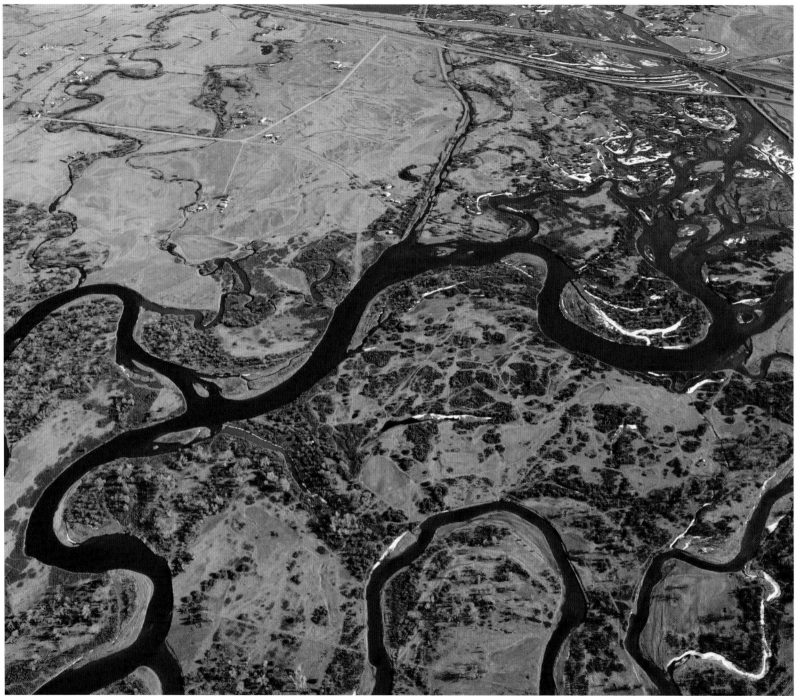

LEFT:

**Missouri River,
Montana, USA**
The headwaters of North
America's longest river rise
in the Rockies of sparsely
populated western Montana.
Along the river's way through
the state, it flows through
the Missouri Breaks (made
famous by the 1976 Marlon
Brando film of the same
name), where water and wind
have carved the badlands into
strange outcrops and bluffs.

OPPOSITE:

**Little Missouri River,
North Dakota, USA**
The Little Missouri flows
through the Theodore
Roosevelt Wilderness before
joining the Missouri River
at Lake Sakakawea. In
1884, Roosevelt established
his Elkhorn Ranch on the
banks of the Little Missouri,
before largely abandoning
it three years later after the
devastatingly hard winter
of 1886–7.

LEFT:

Ohio River, Ohio, USA

The Ohio River courses for 1579km (981 miles) from Pennsylvania to its meeting with the Mississippi River on the southern border of Illinois. For most of its journey, the river and its banks are highly industrialized. In Stratton, Ohio (*pictured*), the water brings barges of coal to a power plant.

ABOVE:

Big Four Bridge, Ohio River, Kentucky–Indiana, USA

Completed in 1895, this six-span truss bridge was formerly used by the Cleveland, Cincinnati, Chicago and St Louis Railway, also known as the Big Four Railroad. After the last train ran across the bridge in 1968, it fell into disuse, before being opened for walkers and cyclists in 2014.

Horseshoe Bend, Colorado River, Arizona, USA

This incised meander of the Colorado River began to form five million years ago when the rock under the river was uplifted by tectonic forces, leaving the river trapped in its bed and eroding deeply into the rock. In a few more million years, the river will cut through the neck of the bend, forming a natural bridge and abandoning the meander for ever.

OPPOSITE:

Hoover Dam, Colorado River, Arizona–Nevada, USA

Having cost the lives of 112 workers to accidents and carbon monoxide poisoning in the diversion tunnels, the Hoover Dam was completed in 1936. Every year, the dam's 17 main turbines provide more than four terawatt-hours of electricity to Nevada, Arizona and California.

LEFT:

**Merced River,
California, USA**
The Merced flows from
the Sierra Nevada into the
San Joaquin Valley, where
it joins the San Joaquin on
its journey to the Pacific
at San Francisco Bay. The
river gained its European
title in 1806 when a Spanish
expedition named it Nuestra
Señora de la Merced ('Our
Lady of Mercy').

RIGHT TOP:

Grijalva River, Mexico
Sumidero Canyon, cut away
by the Grijalva River, is
shadowed by near-vertical
cliffs up to 1000m (3300ft)
high. These limestone walls
hold the fossils of countless
ancient sea creatures.

RIGHT BOTTOM:

**Rio Grande Gorge Bridge,
New Mexico, USA**
The 1965 Gorge Bridge crosses
the Rio Grande near Taos.
It offers a dizzying drop of
183m (600ft) from US Route
64 to the water below.

Central and South America and the Caribbean

This region is home to the queen among rivers, the Amazon, the largest river in the world by volume, carrying 20 per cent of all the world's flowing freshwater. The Amazon is South America's longest river, coursing for 6400km (4000 miles) from the mountains of Peru to the Atlantic Ocean, near the port of Belém in northern Brazil. The Amazon's drainage basin encompasses 6.3 million sq km (2.4 million sq miles), around a third of the South American continent. For thousands of years, the river has provided the peoples of the Amazon with food, drinking water and transport. Today, as Amazon streams are clogged by logs and poisoned by mercury, these ecosystems are under threat.

The river is at the heart of the world's arguments and fears about the destruction that our species wreaks. Fittingly, there are conflicting stories about how the Amazon gained its modern name, whether from a conflict between newcomers and indigenous peoples or from its own, hopefully invincible, nature. Many say the name comes from the fierce female warriors of Greek mythology and was bestowed in 1542 by conquistador Francisco de Orellana, after a skirmish with female (and male) Pira-Tapuya fighters. Others say the name comes from the Tupi or Guarani words for 'boat-breaker', because of the treacherous underwater root systems of the river's plants.

OPPOSITE:
Duaba River, Cuba
In the chocolate-growing region of Baracoa, in eastern Cuba, is El Yunque National Park, where tropical moist broadleaf forests of aguacatillo, andiroba and myrtle line the banks of the Duaba River. The city of Baracoa is said to be on the spot where Columbus landed in 1492.

LEFT:

San Juan River, Nicaragua

Before the construction of the Panama Canal, the San Juan River was a major route from the Atlantic to the Pacific Ocean. From the 1850s, steamships carried travellers up the river, from its mouth on the Caribbean Sea to its source, Lake Nicaragua. From the lake's western shore, stagecoaches took travellers the last 20km (12 miles) to the Pacific Coast.

ABOVE:

Coco River, Nicaragua

In the northern highlands of Nicaragua, the Coco River has carved out the Somoto Canyon. At its narrowest, the 3km (2 mile) gorge is just 10m (33ft) wide and navigable only by swimmers and the disturbed bats that swoop overhead. During the rainy season, flash floods are an ever-present danger for hikers and abseilers.

RIGHT:

Cangrejal River, Honduras
Offering some of the best whitewater rafting in Central America, the Cangrejal surges and tumbles through the Cordillera Nombre de Dios mountains to the Caribbean Sea.

OPPOSITE:

Orinoco Delta, Venezuela
Before the Orinoco River meets the Atlantic Ocean, it splits into countless distributaries, known as *caños*, forming a delta (shown here in a satellite image) that covers 43,646 sq km (16,852 sq miles). This region of swamp forests and mangroves is inhabited by the Warao people, who traditionally live in stilt-supported huts and travel the waterways by canoe.

**Orinoco River,
Colombia–Venezuela**
Along the border between
Venezuela and Colombia, the
Orinoco River foams around
numerous islets and rocks,
forming the Atures Rapids.
The nearby city of Puerto
Ayacucho grew up in the late
19th century to facilitate the
transportation of rubber past
this impossible-to-navigate
portion of the 2250km
(1400 mile) river.

ABOVE:

Fisherman, Amazon River, Brazil

At 6400km (4000 miles) long, the Amazon is the planet's second longest river, after the Nile. More than 30 million people live in the Amazon Basin, among them around 2.7 million who identify as belonging to indigenous groups such as the Yanomami and Kayapo. For thousands of years, these peoples have fished and travelled through the basin in dugout canoes.

RIGHT:

Amazon River, Brazil

Covering 80 per cent of the Amazon Basin, the Amazon Rainforest is home to around 390 billion trees. One in ten of all the world's known species lives in the forest, including more than 3000 fish. Among those species are the notorious red-bellied piranha and the arapaima, which at 3m (9.8ft) long is one of the world's largest freshwater fish.

**Várzea Forest,
Amazon River, Brazil**
The várzea is the Amazon
Basin forest that is seasonally
flooded with whitewater.
Whitewater rivers have high
levels of suspended sediment,
giving the water a close to
neutral pH. During the rainy
season, water levels rise by
up to 15m (49ft), replenishing
nutrients in the soil and
creating a productive breeding
ground for fish.

**Confluence of Rio Negro
and Amazon River, Brazil**
The Lower Amazon begins
just east of the Brazilian city
of Manaus, where the dark
waters of the Rio Negro meet
the sandy Upper Amazon,
known here as the Solimões.
The Rio Negro is a blackwater
river, flowing slowly through
forested swamps and picking
up tannins from decaying
vegetation. The result is water
that looks like black tea.

Juruá River, Brazil
The Juruá is one of the Amazon's longest tributaries, flowing for around 3100km (1925 miles). As shown in this satellite image, for much of its course the Juruá is slow-moving, low-lying and elaborately meandering.

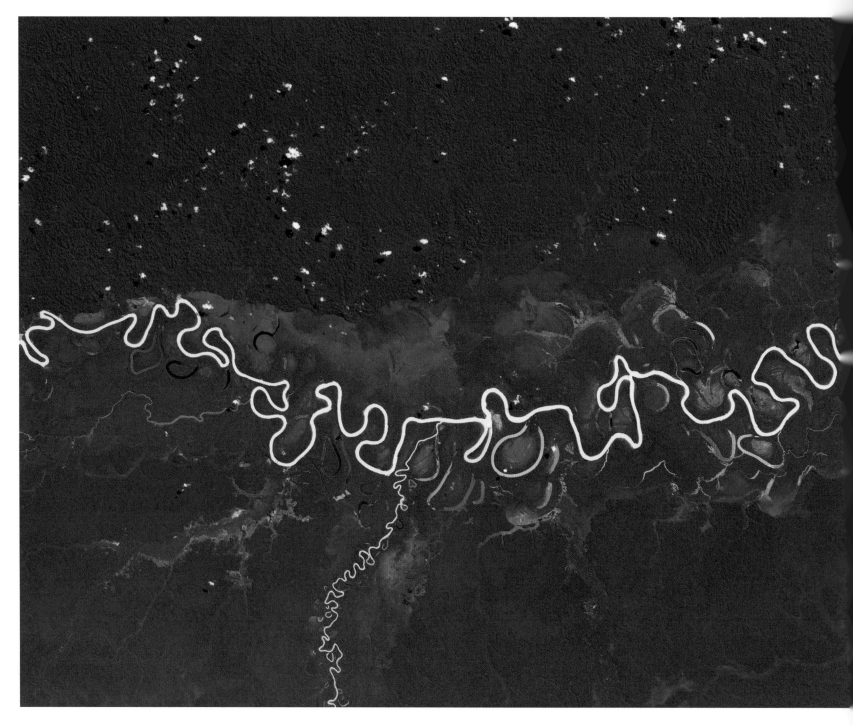

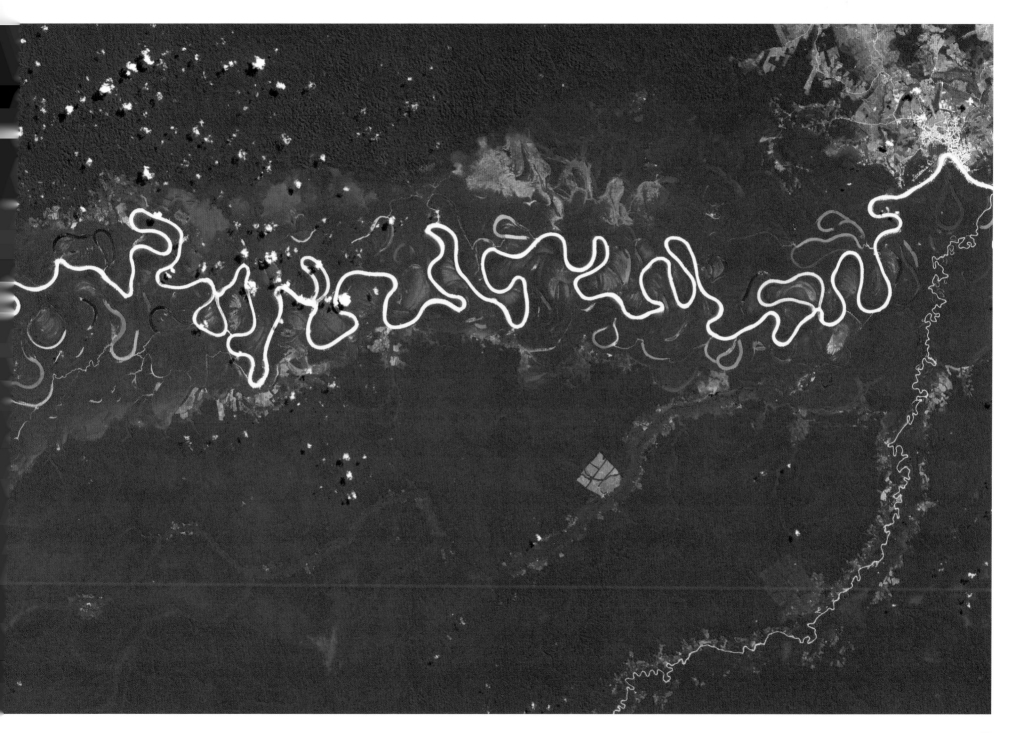

Madeira River, Porto Velho, Brazil
The Madeira is one of the Amazon Basin's most economically active waterways, being used for the transportation of grain, petrol and the mineral cassiterite. The riverside city of Porto Velho is home to half a million people, many of them miners.

ABOVE AND RIGHT:
Iguazu River, Brazil

With its source in southern Brazil, the 1320km (820 mile) Iguazu River is a major tributary of the Paraná River, which it meets 23km (14 miles) downriver from the Iguazu Falls. With a width of 2.7km (1.7 miles) and 150 to 300 waterfalls, the Iguazu Falls are the world's largest group of waterfalls. The falls formed where the Iguazu River surges over the edge of the Paraná Plateau.

LEFT:

Purus River, Brazil
From its headwaters in eastern Peru, the Purus flows for 2960km (1840 miles) before joining the Amazon. In this aerial photograph, several oxbow lakes can be seen, formed when the river eroded through the necks of its meanders, cutting off the bends.

OPPOSITE:

Purus River, Acre, Brazil
Fishing is a major source of income in the Brazilian state of Acre. The catch includes several species of catfish, often known locally as *surubim*; *pacu*, which are close relatives of piranhas; and *matrinchã*, sometimes known as South American trout.

Paraguay River, Brazil
The 2695km (1675 mile)
long Paraguay River courses
through Brazil, Bolivia,
Paraguay and northern
Argentina on its way to meet
the Paraná River. Not yet
dammed for hydroelectricity,
among the South American
rivers the Paraguay is second
only to the Amazon in its
navigable length.

Paraguay River, Pantanal
The largest of the water
lilies, *Victoria amazonica*
has leaves up to 3m (10ft)
across. The plant is native to
the slow-moving bayous of
the Amazon Basin and the
Pantanal. The Paraguay River
is the major waterway of the
Pantanal, the world's largest
tropical wetland.

Xingó Canyon, São Francisco River, Brazil
In 1994, the damming of the São Francisco near Piranhas
created Lake Xingó and flooded the Xingó Canyon and its caves.
The canyon and surrounding region of *caatinga* vegetation are
protected. The *caatinga* is an ecoregion of desert vegetation
characterized by thorny trees, cacti and dry grasses.

Xingó Canyon, São Francisco River, Brazil
Until modern times, boats on the São Francisco were always
adorned with a figurehead carved as a human or animal with
bared fangs, called a *carranca*. These served to frighten away evil
spirits and also to identify tradespeople. Today, *carrancas* are
usually only seen in museums.

LEFT:

Itaipu Dam, Paraná River, Brazil–Paraguay

Completed in 1984, the Itaipu Dam provides four-fifths of Paraguay's electricity and a quarter of Brazil's. The plant's electricity generation is exceeded only by China's Three Gorges Dam. The 196m (643ft) high dam created a vast reservoir that submerged the famous Guairá Falls, which comprised 18 cataracts with a total height of 114m (375ft).

ABOVE:

Paraná River, Brazil

The Paraná gets its name from the Tupi phrase '*para rehe onáva*', which means 'as big as the sea'. This 4880km (3030 mile) river flows from the confluence of the Paranaiba and Rio Grande, in southern Brazil, to its meeting with the Uruguay River. Here the two rivers form the immense Río de la Plata, on the border between Argentina and Uruguay.

BELOW:
**Puerto Falcón Border Crossing,
Pilcomayo River, Argentina–Paraguay**
The meandering course of the Pilcomayo forms much of the border between Argentina and Paraguay. The river probably gets its name from the Quechua words for red ('*pilku*') and river ('*mayu*').

RIGHT:
Sucre Bridge, Pilcomayo River, Bolivia
Built in 1890, this 200m (655ft) long suspension bridge spans the Pilcomayo River near Bolivia's capital, Sucre. The bridge and city were named after Antonio José de Sucre (1795–1830), who fought for independence from Spain at the Battle of Ayacucho and became president of both Peru and Bolivia.

Rio Negro, Pantanal, Brazil
One of several Brazilian
Rio Negros named for their
dark waters, this river flows
through the Pantanal of Mato
Grosso do Sul state in the
southwest. Aerial roots allow
many Pantanal plants to
breathe air in this vast region
of water and sodden soil.

**Tupé Beach, Rio Negro,
Near Manaus, Brazil**
A few kilometres west of
Manaus, a sandbar has
formed where the Tupé River
flows into the Rio Negro. The
beach, accessible only by boat,
is part of the Tupé Sustainable
Development Reserve, which
preserves a region of *igapó*,
an ecosystem where forest is
seasonally flooded with acidic
blackwater rich in tannins.

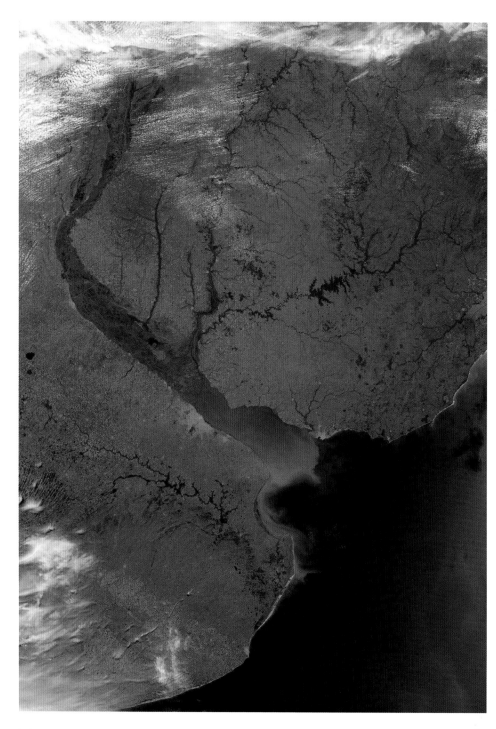

LEFT:

Río de la Plata, Argentina–Uruguay

This satellite image shows the Río de la Plata, as well as the Paraná, Uruguay and Negro Rivers (left to right) stretching to the north. If the Plata is considered a river (it can also be called an estuary), it is the widest in the world, reaching 220km (140 miles) across. River sediments turn the water brown.

RIGHT:

Río de la Plata, Colonia, Uruguay

In the 1520s, while working for Spain, Venetian explorer Sebastian Cabot traded silver with the Guarani around this waterway. The experience prompted him to give the Plata (meaning 'silver') its modern name. It was hope for a wealth of silver that earned the region to the south of the river the name 'Argentina' (from the Italian for silver) among Italian explorers.

Europe

The Volga courses from the forests of northwestern Russia to the Caspian Sea. At 3531km (2194 miles), it is Russia's, and Europe's, longest river. In the Russian consciousness, the Volga is more than a river: it is *Volga-Matushka* ('Mother Volga'). The river has played a central role in Russian culture, from the folktale *Volga and Vazuza*, about two competing rivers, to Ilya Repin's 1873 painting *Barge Haulers on the Volga*, an influential condemnation of social inequality; from the 1938 comedy film *Volga-Volga* to the rousing 1965 drama, *The Bridge is Built*. The river's importance lies partly in its long history as an essential trade artery, carrying merchants from Scandinavia to the Caspian Sea and the Byzantine Empire or beyond. Astrakhan, on the river's delta, was Russia's medieval gateway to the eastern markets of Persia and India. Catherine the Great saw the Volga as the dividing line between the 'West' and 'Asia'. Far from being a dividing line, the Volga and its many-armed tributaries have long been a confluence. In 1942–3, the Volga was indeed a dividing line during the battle for Stalingrad (today known as Volgograd), as Stalin ordered: 'Not a step back!' The Germans hoped to cut the vital Volga supply line of Caucasus oil to central Russia. The devastating German defeat at Stalingrad was a turning point not just on the Eastern Front but for the whole war.

OPPOSITE:

Aldford Iron Bridge, River Dee, England
Completed in 1824, this cast iron bridge was designed by the great Scottish civil engineer Thomas Telford (1757–1834). Its single arch is 50m (164ft) wide. Telford's groundbreaking use of lightweight cast iron arches allowed bridge spans longer than was possible in stone.

BELOW:
Flooded River Ouse, York, England
In February 2020, the River Ouse overflowed its banks in York. The city has known floods throughout its long history, but they have been far more frequent in the 21st century. Heavy rainfall in the Ouse's drainage basin, which covers a large part of the North Yorkshire Moors, Pennines and Dales, results in flooding across the low-lying land from York south to Selby.

RIGHT:
River Great Ouse, Ely, England
The Great Ouse is one of many English rivers called Ouse, a name that comes from the Celtic word for 'water'. This Ouse flows from Buckinghamshire to the North Sea near Kings Lynn, Norfolk. Much of its course has been channelized to facilitate barges and reduce the risk of flooding. The river and its tributaries are navigable for 255km (158 miles).

**River Severn,
Purton Hulks, England**

At Purton Hulks, there is just 50m (160ft) between the River Severn and the Gloucester and Sharpness Canal. In 1909, after a collapse in the riverbank threatened to make the canal unnavigable, the canal's chief engineer ordered the grounding of old vessels to reinforce the river's banks.

OPPOSITE:
**River Severn,
Shrewsbury, England**

Since the late 1990s, the market town of Shrewsbury has faced regular flooding from the River Severn. Despite the erection of flood defences in 2003, the town centre was badly flooded once more in 2020, damaging countless homes and businesses.

RIGHT:

Monmouth Viaduct, River Wye, Wales

The 1861 Monmouth Viaduct carried the Coleford, Monmouth, Usk and Pontypool Railway over the Wye. Today, only its red sandstone arches remain, while the two steel lattice girder spans over the river have been removed.

OPPOSITE:

Mill Street Weir, Ludlow, River Teme, England

The first weirs were built in Ludlow in the 13th century to harness the power of the Teme's waters for the settlement's many mills. Before the weirs tamed the river, its noisy rushing earned the town its name, which means 'loud hill' in Old English.

FAR LEFT:

Tower Bridge, River Thames, London, England
Completed in 1894, Tower Bridge is a suspension and bascule bridge, with counterweights to balance the upward swing of its moving sections. The bascules are raised to 86° for boat traffic. The original raising mechanism was powered by pressurized water, today replaced by oil.

LEFT TOP:

Thames Barrier, Silvertown–Charlton, River Thames, England
The Thames Barrier was constructed in 1974–82 to protect the London floodplain from inundation. The gates, which span a 520m (1710ft) wide stretch of the River Thames, are closed during North Sea storm surges and particularly high tides.

LEFT BOTTOM:

Cookham, River Thames, England
Flowing for 346km (215 miles) from Thames Head in Gloucestershire to the Thames Estuary, the Thames is the longest river wholly in England. It is just 8km (5 miles) shorter than the United Kingdom's longest river, the Severn, which rises in Wales.

BELOW:

Aughinish Refinery, Shannon River, Ireland

Located on the peninsula of Aughinish in the Shannon Estuary, Europe's largest bauxite refinery takes deliveries of South American buaxite from its deep-water jetties. The plant produces alumina, which will be processed into aluminium. Nearby, in an abandoned quarry, is Ireland's first butterfly sanctuary, where dingy skippers and small blues can be spotted.

RIGHT:

McDermott's Castle, Lough Key, Boyle River, Ireland

The Boyle flows from Lough Gara to Lough Key, then on to meet the Shannon near Carrick-on-Shannon. Lough Key is named after Cé, a druid of the god Nuada, who was the first king of the Tuatha Dé Danann. After Cé died, the lake is said to have poured out from his grave. The lake's Castle Island has been the site of a castle since the 12th century.

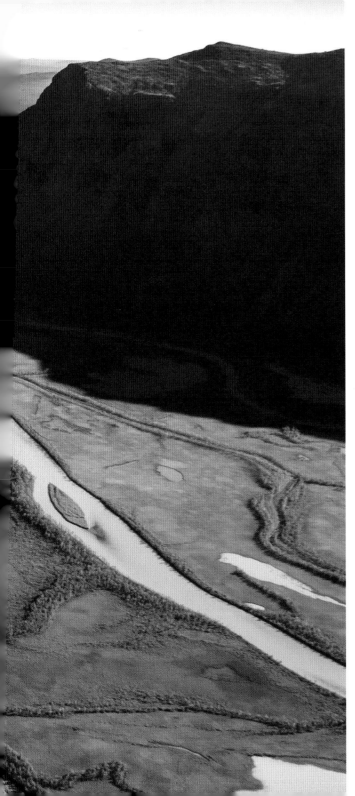

LEFT:

Rapa River Delta, Sweden
In Lapland, at the mouth of Lake Laitaure, the Rapa River forms an elaborate delta as it flows through a trough valley. The river carries ice-cold water and thousands of tons of sediment from around 30 glaciers on and around Sarektjåkkå, the second highest mountain in Sweden.

ABOVE:

Namsen River, Norway
The Namsen is renowned for its Atlantic salmon, which journey upriver to spawn. Salmon caught here regularly weigh more than 20kg (44lb). One method of fishing on this river is harling: anglers, operating two or three rods, sit in a rowing boat that gently floats downstream.

BELOW:

Driel Weir, Rhine River, Netherlands

The Rhine flows for 1230km (760 miles) from the lake of Tomasee, in Switzerland's Lepontine Alps, to the North Sea. Near Driel, a weir serves to distribute the river's water across its branches. When the weir is closed, much of the Rhine's water flows into the IJssel and on into the IJsselmeer, ensuring that water levels remain sufficient on that key shipping route.

OPPOSITE:

Château de Chenonceau, Cher River, France

In 1514–22, this Renaissance château was built on the banks of the Cher. Later in the century, the palace was extended across the river by Henri II's mistress Diane de Poitiers and, later, by his widow, Catherine de' Medici. The Cher's source is in the Massif Central, from where the 368km (229 mile) river flows to join the Loire near the city of Tours.

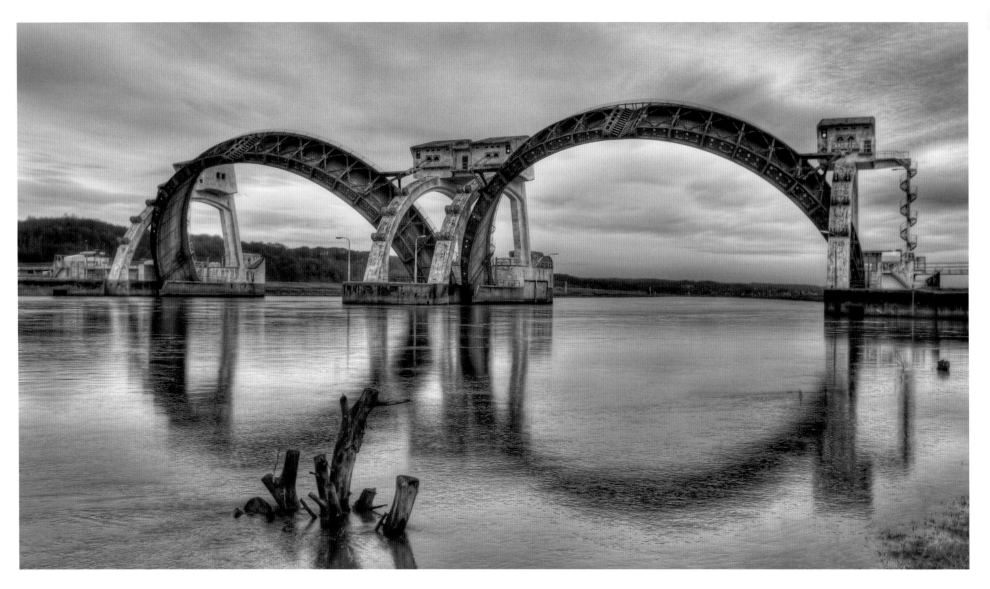

FAR LEFT:
Beynac-et-Cazenac, Dordogne River, France
Perched on a limestone cliff, the Château de Beynac guards the town of Beynac-et-Cazenac and the Dordogne below. The Barons of Beynac built the castle's Romanesque keep in the 12th century. During the Hundred Years' War, Beynac stayed in French hands, while Castelnaud, on the river's opposite bank, was held by the English.

LEFT:
Libourne, Dordogne River, France
Libourne lies at the confluence of the Isle and Dordogne Rivers. The river's mouth is the Gironde Estuary, where the incoming tide can form a wave, a phenomenon known as a tidal bore or *mascaret*.

LEFT:

Avignon, Rhône River, France

Built in 1234, the famous Pont d'Avignon bridge originally had 22 arches, now just four survive. It was abandoned in the 17th century due to damage from the Rhône's frequent floods. The song '*Sur le Pont d'Avignon*' describes summer dances under (not, in fact, '*sur*') the bridge on the Rhône's Ile de la Barthelasse.

RIGHT:

Garonne River and Gironde Estuary, France

The source of the Garonne is just over the Spanish border, in the Aran Valley of the Pyrenees. The river travels northwestward to reach the Atlantic Ocean at the Gironde Estuary, a little north of the city of Bordeaux. The Garonne is rich with detritic sediment, which nurtures the *terroirs* of the famous Bordeaux wine region.

**Grangent Dam,
Loire River, France**
Built between 1955 and 1957,
the Grangent Dam generates
hydroelectric power and
regulates the Loire's flow to
avoid flooding. The concrete
arch dam is 55m (180ft) high
and 206m (676ft) wide.

Nantes, Loire River, France
The city of Nantes lies on
both banks of the Loire and
on the Île de Nantes, in the
centre of the river. Until the
early 20th century, the island
was divided into several islets,
but the intervening river
channels were filled and water
diverted, transforming the
urban landscape. Today, the
island is linked to the rest of
the city by 13 bridges.

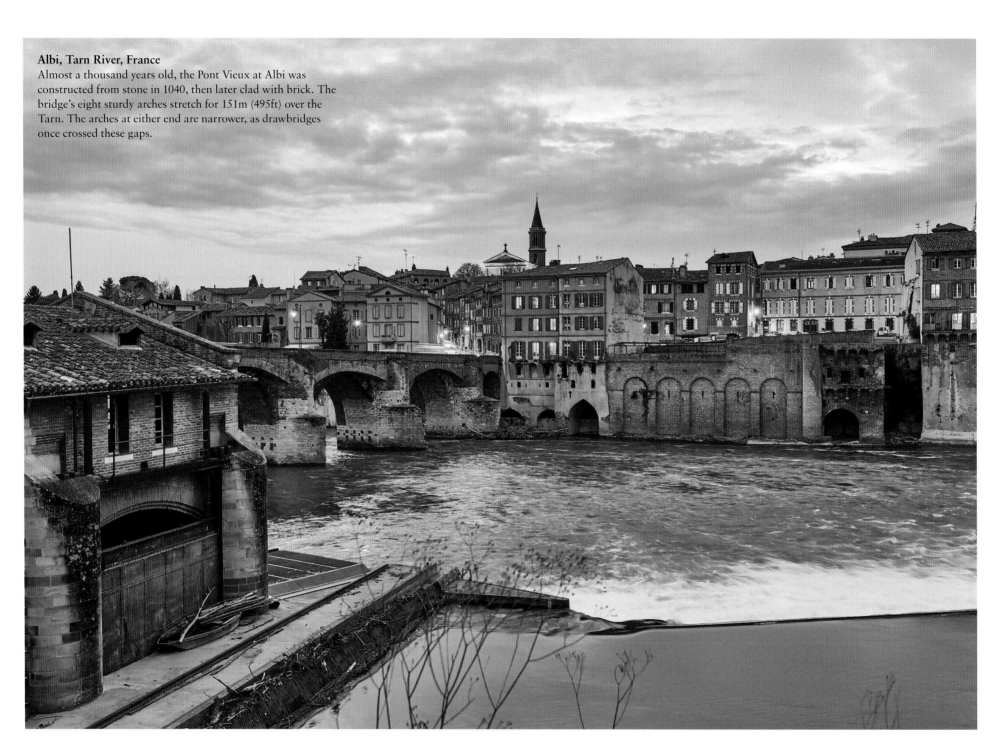

Albi, Tarn River, France
Almost a thousand years old, the Pont Vieux at Albi was constructed from stone in 1040, then later clad with brick. The bridge's eight sturdy arches stretch for 151m (495ft) over the Tarn. The arches at either end are narrower, as drawbridges once crossed these gaps.

Île de la Cité, Paris, Seine River, France
The Île de la Cité, site of the medieval city of Paris, is one of two natural islands on the Seine within Paris, the other being the Île Saint-Louis. A third island, Île aux Cygnes, was built in 1827 to protect the old Pont de Grenelle. There are 37 bridges over the Seine within Paris, eight linking the Île de la Cité.

RIGHT:

Rouen, Seine River, France

The Seine is navigable by ocean-going vessels for 120km (75 miles) from the English Channel, as far as Rouen. The port of Rouen, just downstream from the city centre and its cathedral, is the fifth largest in France.

OPPOSITE TOP:

Vernon, Seine River, France

In Normandy's Vernon, a 16th-century timbered mill rests on a ruined bridge. In the 16th century, this was one of five flour mills that had taken over the 12th-century bridge. They were powered by water wheels that could be raised and lowered between the bridge's piers depending on water level.

OPPOSITE BOTTOM:

Pont de Normandie, Seine River, France

A 2143m (7032ft) bridge links Le Havre with Honfleur. When the bridge opened in 1995, it was the longest cable-stayed bridge in the world, a record lost four years later to Japan's Tatara Bridge.

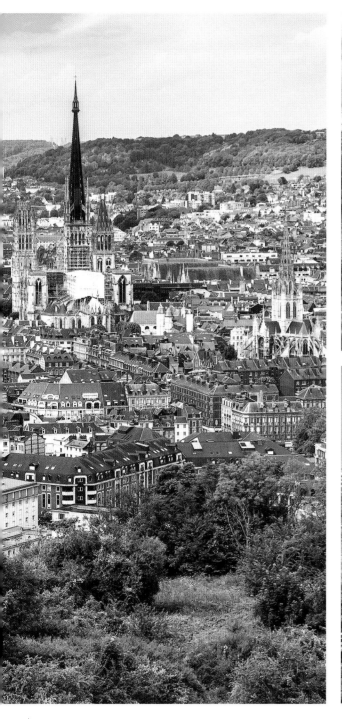

LEFT:
Duero River, Arribes del Duero Natural Park, Spain
From its source in the Picos de Urbión, the Duero meanders westwards, across Spain and northern Portugal. For 112km (70 miles), the river and its canyons form the border between Spain and Portugal.

ABOVE:
Ribarroja Dam, Ebro River, Spain
Completed in 1969, the Ribarroja gravity dam impounds the Ebro, which at 930km (580 miles) is the longest river entirely within the borders of Spain. The Ribarroja is one of three major dams constructed on the Ebro in Catalonia.

ABOVE:

Aldeadávila Dam, Duero River, Spain
There are 15 dams along the Duero, which becomes known as the Duoro once it enters Portugal. Aldeadávila, a concrete arch gravity dam, is one of five along the border between the two countries, two of them owned by Spain. The 140m (460ft) high dam supplies water to Spain's largest power station.

RIGHT:

Porto, Douro River, Portugal
The Douro reaches the Atlantic Ocean at the city of Porto, which was first settled in the third century BCE. Central Porto lies on the north side of the Douro Estuary, its colourful Baroque buildings spilling down the hillside to the busy quays. For many centuries, this was where barges unloaded their cargo of wine.

RIGHT:

Tiber Island, Rome, Tiber River, Italy

As the Tiber flows through Rome, little Tiber Island, just 270m (890ft) long and 67m (220ft) wide, nestles in a meander. From the third century BCE, the island was associated with healing as the site of a temple to Asclepius, Greek god of medicine. In keeping with the tradition, the Fatebenefratelli Hospital has been operating on the island since the 16th century.

OPPOSITE TOP:

Rome, Tiber River, Italy

In this satellite image of Rome and environs, the Tiber can be seen winding from the northeast of the city to the southwest, where it enters the Tyrrhenian Sea between Fiumicino and the modern town of Ostia.

OPPOSITE BOTTOM:

Drava River, Croatia

The Drava flows for 710km (440 miles) through Italy, Austria, Slovenia and Hungary to meet the Danube at Osijek in Croatia. Gravel bars have been deposited by the river mid-stream. Such bars are growing less common on rivers worldwide due to dam-building and gravel extraction.

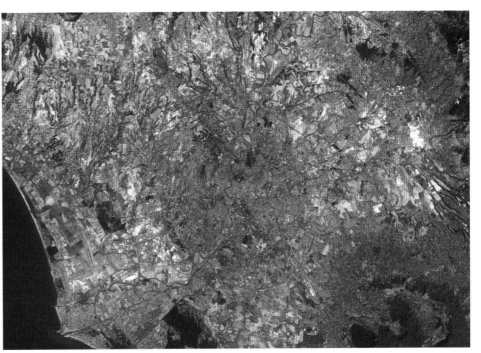

OPPOSITE:

Rhône Glacier, Switzerland
The 7km (4mile) long Rhône
Glacier is the source of the
Rhône River, which travels
813km (505 miles) through
Switzerland and France. At
Arles, in southern France,
the river splits into two arms,
forming the Camargue Delta.

RIGHT:

**Rhine Falls, High Rhine
River, Switzerland**
Around 150m (490ft) wide
and with a drop of 23m (75ft),
this waterfall on the Rhine is
the most powerful in Europe
by average flow rate. The falls
formed 14,000 to 17,000 years
ago as erosion-resistant rocks
on either side of the river
channel narrowed its path.

RIGHT TOP:

Aggstein Castle, Danube River, Austria

Impregnable on its outcrop, 12th-century Aggstein Castle has clear views down the Danube. The castle was never stormed by force, but its inhabitants were occasionally starved out by siege.

OPPOSITE:

Barl, Moselle River, Germany

Barl lies on a meander of the Moselle which rises in the Vosges Mountains of France, then flows through Luxembourg to meet the Rhine at Koblenz, Germany. The slopes around Barl are planted with Riesling grapes.

Rhine River

The Rhine forms part of the Swiss-Liechtenstein, Swiss-Austrian, Swiss-German and Franco-German borders, then journeys through Germany and the Netherlands to the North Sea. During World War II, the Rhine was a formidable barrier to the Allies. Attempts to cross were immortalized in the films *The Bridge at Remagen* (1969) and *A Bridge too Far* (1977).

Mannheim Harbour, Rhine River, Germany

The river port of Mannheim, at the confluence of the Rhine and Neckar, processes more than eight million tonnes of containers every year. The most frequent destinations from Mannheim are Rotterdam (which lies on the Rhine–Meuse–Scheldt Delta), Stuttgart (via the Neckar River) and Antwerp (via the Rhine and the Scheldt–Rhine Canal).

LEFT:

Bratislava, Danube River, Slovakia

The Danube courses through more countries (10) than any other river on its 2850km (1770 mile) journey from Germany to the Black Sea. As the Danube passes Bratislava, it forms the border between Austria and Slovakia, then between Slovakia and Hungary. Bratislava is the only national capital that borders two other countries.

ABOVE:

Wisłoujscie Fortress, Vistula River, Poland

The longest river in Poland, the Vistula runs for 1047km (651 miles) from the Barania Góra mountain to the Baltic Sea. In the port of Gdansk, a branch of the Vistula known as the Martwa Wisła (meaning 'Dead Vistula', due to its slow flow) runs past the four-bastion Wisłoujscie Fortress, with its 1482 lighthouse tower that once guarded port traffic.

**Budapest, Danube River,
Hungary**

The Danube splits the
Hungarian capital in two:
hilly Buda (on the left) and
larger, flatter Pest. The first
settlement here was founded
by the Celts in the first century
BCE, on Gellért Hill in Buda.
In 106 CE, the town became
capital of the Roman province
of Pannonia Inferior.

OPPOSITE:

**Visegrád, Danube River,
Hungary**

The castle of Visegrád has
kept watch over the Danube
Bend and Börzsöny Hills
since the 13th century. This
photogenic U-shaped bend in
the Danube earns the region
its name. Here the river
follows the edge of a caldera
formed during an eruption
around 15 million years ago.

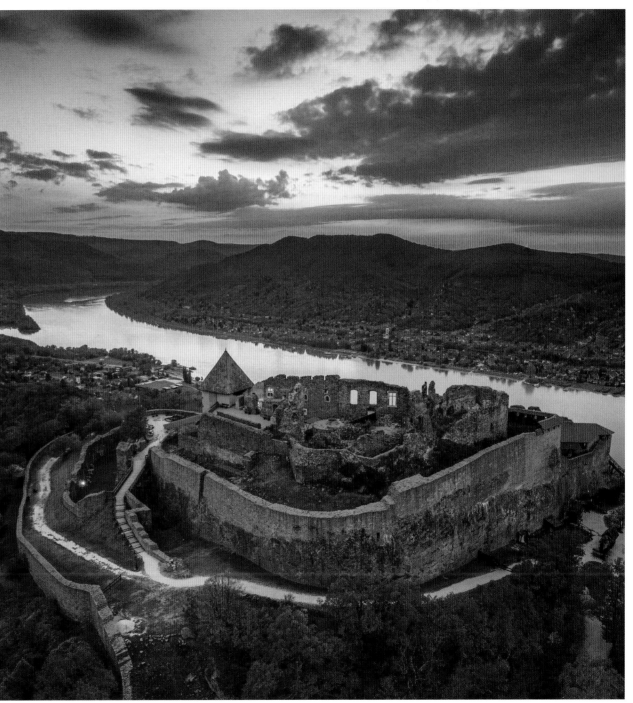

Soca River, Slovenia
The Soca runs from Slovenia's Julian Alps to the Gulf of Trieste near the Italian town of Monfalcone. The river Soca inspired Slovenian poet Simon Gregorcic (1844–1906) to write his patriotic ode 'Soci': 'You are magnificent, limpid daughter of the heights! You are graceful in your natural beauty …'

Sava River, Croatia
A village nestles against the banks of an oxbow lake close to the Sava River. Once part of a meandering curve, an oxbow lake forms from the remnants of a river after silt and sediment has built up on the inner bank; over many centuries, the neck of the bend narrows and eventually closes off.

LEFT:

Dobruja, Danube River, Romania
Before the Danube fans into its vast delta, the river snakes over the windy plateau of Dobruja, in eastern Romania. Most people in this region are farmers, growing grapes and grains and raising cattle. The region probably takes its name from a 14th-century despot named Dobrotitsa.

OPPOSITE:

Devil's Bridge, Arda River, Bulgaria
This 16th-century footbridge across the Arda is said to be on the site of a Roman bridge on the route that linked the Aegean Sea with the province of Thrace. Across Europe, dozens of similar stone arched bridges are known as 'Devil's Bridge', as their engineering achievement prompted people to believe that the devil must have lent a hand.

Loobu River, Lahemaa National Park, Estonia

The Loobu meanders for just 62km (39 miles) through northern Estonia before draining into the Gulf of Finland, the eastern arm of the Baltic Sea. The forested Lahemaa National Park boasts many raised bogs, highly acidic environments fed only by rainfall.

LEFT TOP:

Zvartes Rock, Amata River, Latvia

The swiftly flowing Amata is fringed by cliffs of Devonian red sandstone. The most famous of these is Zvartes Rock, said to be the meeting place of witches on special occasions such as Whitsunday and the Nativity of St John the Baptist. The story goes that the 20m (66ft) height of the rock forces them to use their broomsticks.

LEFT BOTTOM:

Berezina River, Naliboki Forest, Belarus

The pine forest and swamps of Naliboki lie between the Biarezina and Neman Rivers. Large mammals found here include bears, deer, wild boars, elks, beavers and bison.

OPPOSITE:

St Vladimir Monument, Dnieper River, Ukraine

A statue of St Vladimir (c.958–1015), who was instrumental in Christianizing the Kievan Rus', stands on the bank of the Dnieper in Kiev. From ancient times, the 2200km (1368 mile) river was part of the Amber Road, along which amber was carried from the Baltic to the Black Sea.

LEFT:

Amur River, Khabarovsk, Russia

After rising in north-central China, the Amur forms the border between Siberian Russia and China for many hundreds of kilometres. Before the 1858 Treaty of Aigun, the border ran far to the north, through the Stanavoy Range.

Chuya River, Russia
The Chuya River wriggles across the steppe of the same name, a 70km (43 mile) long depression formed by plate movements. This sparsely inhabited region, where the temperature ranges from -60°C (-76°F) to 30°C (86°F), continues to be violently shaken by tectonic activity. The Chuya fills many small lakes in the basin, some of them high in mineral salts.

Lena Pillars, Lena River, Russia
Along the banks of the Lena, in eastern Siberia, are weathered
pillars up to 100m (328ft) high, composed of limestone,
marlstone, dolomite and slate, with slate forming the oldest
and bottom layer. The gullies between the pillars were formed
by freeze-thaw action along joints, followed by removal of the
debris by water.

RIGHT TOP:

Ob River, Russia

The world's seventh longest
river runs for 3700km
(2300 miles) through western
Siberia. The navigable
waterways within the Ob
basin reach a length of 15,000
km (9300 miles), forming vital
trade and communication
links, particularly before the
completion of the Trans-
Siberian Railway in 1916.

RIGHT BOTTOM:

Pyshma River, Russia

The Pyshma flows eastwards
from the Urals across the
Western Siberian Plain, where
winters are long and harsh.
The river is frozen over from
November to April.

FAR RIGHT:

Don River, Russia

With its mouth in the Sea of
Azov, which is connected to
the Black Sea by the Strait
of Kerch, the Don has long
been vital to traders, from
the ancient Greeks and
Byzantines to modern anchovy
processors. Since 1952, the
Don has been linked with the
Volga River and the Caspian
Sea by the Volga–Don Canal.

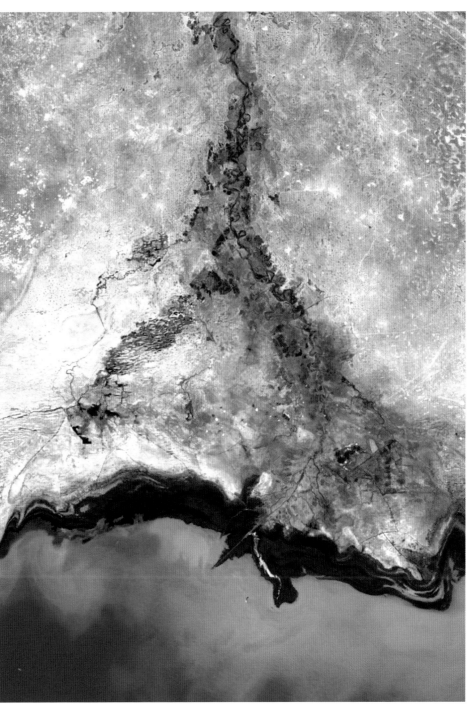

FAR LEFT:
Neva River, St Petersburg, Russia

The Neva flows from Lake Ladoga to the Gulf of Finland at St Petersburg. In the 1240 Battle of the Neva, Scandinavian armies tried to take control of the river and the town of Ladoga. These were vital points on the lucrative trade route between Scandinavia and the Byzantine Empire, via the Neva, Lake Ladoga and the Volkhov, Lovat and Dnieper Rivers.

LEFT:
Ural Delta, Kazakhstan

The Ural, which flows from Russia's Ural Mountains to the Caspian Sea in Kazakhstan, is conventionally considered the boundary between Europe and Asia. The river is a breeding ground for six species of Caspian Sea sturgeon. These fish are critically endangered because of overfishing for their caviar.

LEFT TOP AND BOTTOM:

Volga River,
Near Samara, Russia
In winter, the temperature in
Samara sinks as low as -43°C
(-45°F), allowing the Volga to
be crossed on foot. The river
is free of ice for 200 days a
year, during which time it is a
busy transport corridor to the
Caspian Sea and its oilfields.

RIGHT:

Volga Delta, Russia
Europe's longest river,
the Volga flows 3531km
(2194 miles) from the Valdai
Hills, between St Petersburg
and Moscow, to the Caspian
Sea. The action of wind and
water across the vast Volga
Delta has formed linear dunes
of clay sands, edged with
depressions called ilmens.

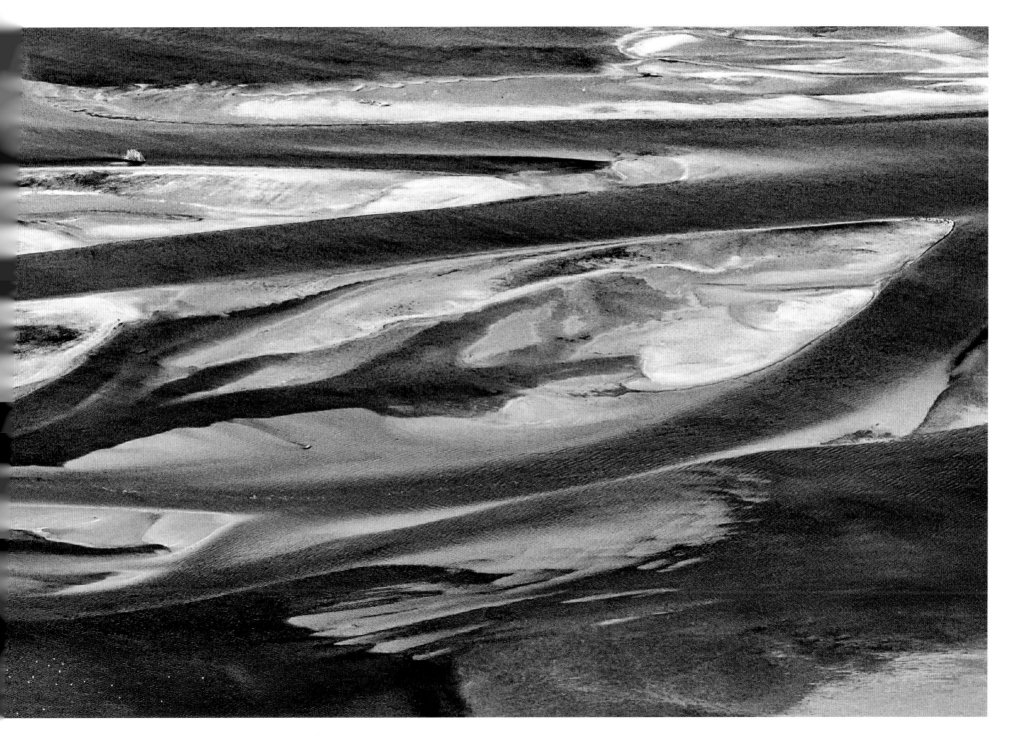

Africa and the Middle East

The world's longest river according to most authorities, the Nile, flows for 6650km (4130 miles) from Rwanda or Burundi in the Great Lakes region to the Mediterranean Sea on Egypt's north coast. Without the wealth brought by the river, the extraordinary civilization of Ancient Egypt, its pyramids and temples, would never have existed. In Egypt's dry desert land, the river supplied drinking water for people and livestock. Its annual overflowing deposited silt, making the land green and fertile. Here, the Egyptians grew crops such as flax, wheat and papyrus, which their boats carried upstream to trade. The river was central to ancient Egyptians' spiritual life. They believed the river's cycle was controlled by the pharoah and the god Hapi. The east bank – where the Sun rose – represented birth; while the west, home to Giza's pyramid tombs and Luxor's Valley of the Kings, was the place of death. Time itself was based on the Nile's cycle, with the calendar having three seasons: Akhet, the time of floods; Peret, the growing season; and Shemu, the low-water harvest. Today, this cycle is less certain, as climate change and upstream dam-building reduce the Nile's flow through Egypt. Since 1999, the Nile Basin Initiative has sought co-operation between the 10 countries that share the Nile, all of them desiring their portion of the socioeconomic benefits that the river's waters offer.

OPPOSITE:
Bourke's Luck Potholes, Treur River, South Africa
Where the Treur plunges into the Blyde River, whirlpools (known as kolks) have worn away circular potholes in the rock. The feature is named after Bernard Thomas Bourke, who in the 1880s correctly predicted that gold would one day be found here, although he was not lucky enough to find any himself.

LEFT:

Bylde/Motlatse River Canyon, South Africa

This river received its European name, which means 'happy' in Old Dutch, when a party of lost Voortrekkers were found safe and well here in 1844. The waterway's pre-European name is Motlatse, meaning 'permanent' in Northern Sotho.

RIGHT:

Limpopo River, Mozambique

The Limpopo flows for 1750km (1087 miles) in a great arc across South Africa to the Indian Ocean on the coast of Mozambique. The river's lower stretches reflect seasonal rainfall patterns, alternating between floods and muddy channels. In 2000, the Limpopo, Incomati and Umbeluzi Rivers burst their banks, causing the deaths of an estimated 800 people.

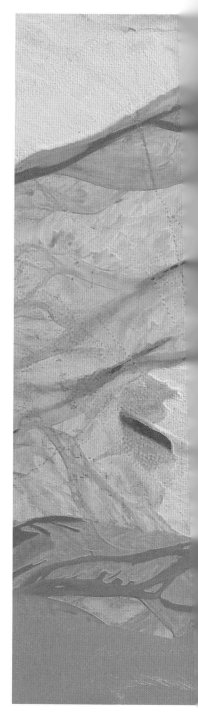

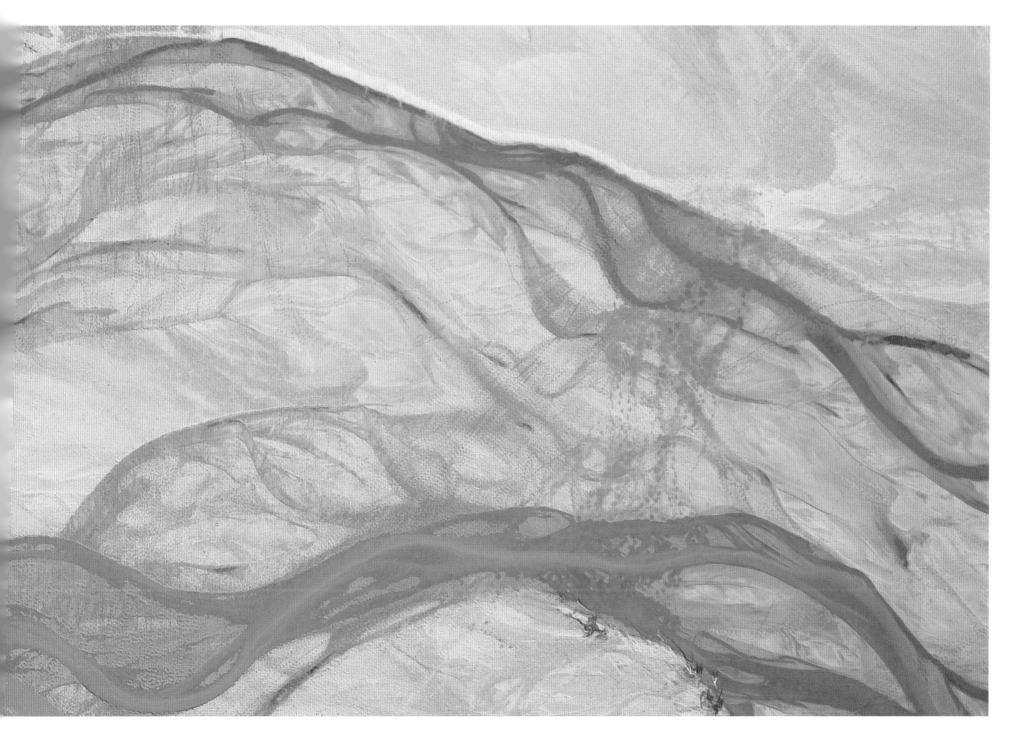

LEFT:

Khwai River, Botswana

The Khwai flows through the Moremi Game Reserve, known for its hippos, African wild dogs, lions and bush elephants. The creation of the reserve in 1963 was championed by Elizabeth Moremi, queen of the Batawana. Today, local people are working on a sustainable development program for the area.

ABOVE:

Okavango Delta, Botswana

Formed where the Okavango River flows into a vast trough, the Okavango Delta encompasses 20,235 sq km (7,813 sq miles) of waterways, swamps and salt islands. This inland delta receives 11 trillion litres (2.9 trillion gallons) of water annually, most of which either evaporates or is lost through plant transpiration.

Victoria Falls, Zambezi River, Zambia–Zimbabwe
The world's largest sheet of falling water is formed where the Zambezi drops over a 108m (355ft) cliff into the First Gorge. From here, the river surges through a gap just 110m (360ft) wide, entering a zigzagging series of further gorges.

Victoria Falls, Zambezi River
Upstream from the Victoria Falls, the Zambezi flows over a wide sheet of basalt, dotted with islands. It was from one of these islands that Scottish missionary David Livingstone saw the falls in 1855, bestowing their English name. The falls are known as *Mosi-oa-Tunya* ('The Smoke That Thunders') in Lozi and *Shungu Namutitima* ('Boiling Water') in Tonga.

LEFT:

Congo River, Yangambi, Democratic Republic of the Congo

The Democratic Republic of the Congo and the Republic of the Congo are named after this deep river, which flows for 4370km (2720 miles) and is second only to the Amazon in the volume of its flow. With few paved roads and railways in this rainforest region, the river is a vital economic and social lifeline. Short journeys are often taken by dugout pirogue.

ABOVE:

Niger River, Niamey, Niger

The capital of Niger lies on the river of the same name, both country and river possibly taking their title from the Berber phrase *ger-n-ger*, meaning 'river of rivers'. The Kennedy Bridge is the main river crossing point in Niamey and has, since 1970, allowed the city's residential neighbourhoods and university to expand onto the western bank (*pictured*).

OPPOSITE TOP AND BOTTOM:

Paraa Ferry, White Nile River, Uganda
This stretch of the White Nile, between Lake Victoria and Lake Albert, is known as the Victoria Nile; after Lake Albert, the river becomes the Albert Nile. The White Nile is one of the two main tributaries of the Nile, along with the shorter Blue Nile. The White Nile is considered to be the headwaters of the Nile, with its ultimate source either in Burundi or Rwanda.

LEFT:

Murchison Falls National Park, White Nile River, Uganda
Uganda's biggest national park is home to a population of bush elephants. With a mature elephant needing up to 190 litres (50 gallons) of water per day, the Nile and its wetlands are essential to survival.

Blue Nile Falls, Blue Nile River, Ethiopia
Around 30km (19 miles) downstream from the source of
the Blue Nile in Lake Tana, the river plunges over a 52m
(170ft) cliff. Since 2010, a weir and dam near Lake Tana have
regulated the falls' dry–wet season variation, but taken away
much of the power that earned them the name *Tis Abay* in
Amharic, meaning 'Great Smoke'.

**White Nile River, Near Juba,
South Sudan**
Before the Second Sudanese Civil War, Juba was a major river
port, as the southern terminus of much traffic along the White
Nile. Today, water pollution and security are major issues here.
When the river floods, it passes over fields that have been used as
latrines, resulting in frequent outbreaks of cholera.

ABOVE:

Nile River, Khartoum, Sudan

Khartoum lies at the confluence of the Blue and White Niles, dividing the city into three parts: central Khartoum, Omdurman and Bahri. There was little more than a fishing village and ferry here before 1821, when the city was founded by Ibrahim Pasha of Egypt, but it was an ideal spot with drinking water, mud for bricks and alluvial soil for the fields.

RIGHT:

Nile River, Egypt

The Egyptians have dug irrigation canals since perhaps 3000 BCE, enlarging the strip of riverside land that it is possible to cultivate in this otherwise desert region. There is currently huge investment in lining Egypt's canals as water conservation becomes a yet more pressing issue due to the Nile's reduction in flow as a result of climate change and upstream dams.

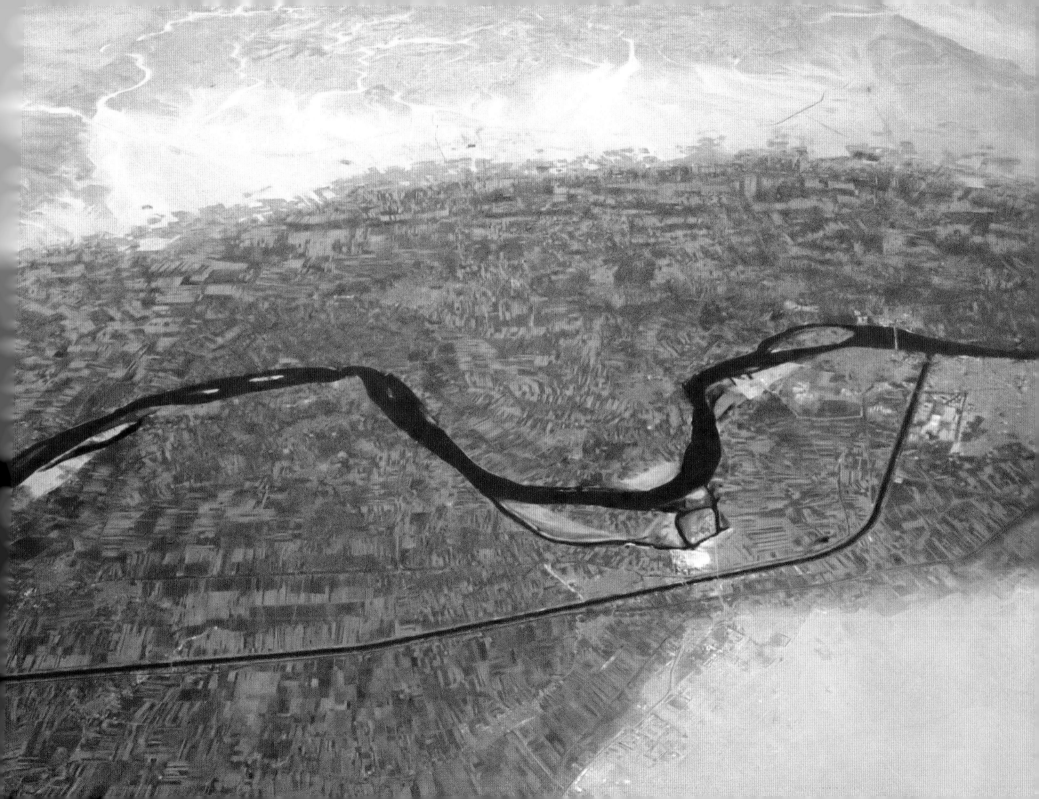

RIGHT:

Felucca, Nile River, Egypt
The earliest boats on the Nile were reed rowing boats. By 3000 BCE, the Egyptians were building square-sailed boats from wood. Designed for shallow waters, the lateen-sailed felucca does not have a keel but a central plate that can be raised over sandbars.

OPPOSITE TOP:

Map of Cairo and the Nile River, Egypt
Cairo was founded by the Fatimids in 969 CE, but the ruins of the ancient city of Memphis are within Greater Cairo. Until the 19th century, when the river was controlled by dams and levees, the waterway was prone to both flooding and shifting westward.

OPPOSITE BOTTOM:

Aswan High Dam, Nile River, Egypt
Before the building of the Aswan High Dam from 1960–70, the Nile's low-water years resulted in drought and hunger, while high-water years could wash away the crops. The dam's reservoir storage of 132 cu km (32 cu miles) increased Egypt's irrigated area by a third.

FAR LEFT:
View from Cairo Tower, Nile River, Egypt
Egypt's tallest structure, Cairo Tower, stands on the Nile's Zamalek Island. Today it is home to some of Cairo's wealthiest neighbourhoods, but the island was under water until the 14th century, when it emerged as three islets.

LEFT:
Nile Delta and River, Egypt
For thousands of years, the Nile Delta has been a rich agricultural region, its fields powering Lower Egypt's ascendance. Since the construction of the Aswan Dam, the delta has seen a reduced flow of sediments and nutrients, resulting in greater use of fertilizers and significant loss of land to the Mediterranean Sea.

LEFT:

Jordan River, Yardenit, Israel

The stretch of the Jordan just south of the Sea of Galilee is a baptismal site that draws hundreds of thousands of Christian pilgrims every year. The river is important to both Christians and Jews, as the place where Jesus was baptized by John the Baptist and where the Israelites crossed into the Promised Land.

RIGHT:

Jordan River and the Dead Sea, West Bank, Israel and Jordan

Both the West Bank and Jordan take their name from the 251km (156 mile) river. In this arid region, the Jordan's importance as a water source is immense and was a contributory factor to the 1967 Six-Day War. Today, Israel is more reliant on desalinated water from the Mediterranean, while Jordan's share of the river's water is regulated by a 1994 peace treaty.

**Karanlik Canyon,
Karasu River, Turkey**

Its name meaning 'Dark Canyon', the Karanlik was carved out by the Karasu, one of the sources of the Euphrates. Today, the confluence of the two rivers is the reservoir of the Keban Dam, built in 1966–74. The Karasu rises on the snow-covered slopes of Mount Dumlu in northeastern Turkey, the spring thaw multiplying the river's flow.

**Atatürk Dam Lake,
Euphrates River, Turkey**

The 1992 Atatürk Dam created a reservoir with a surface area of 817 sq km (315 sq miles), making it the country's third largest lake. Irrigation supplied by the lake has increased local cotton production by 60 per cent.

LEFT:

Old Bridge, Hasankeyf, Tigris River, Turkey
This ruined bridge across the Tigris was built between 1147 and 1167 by the Artuqid Turkmens, before finally collapsing in the 17th century. This photograph was taken shortly before the bridge and the ancient town of Hasankeyf were submerged by the completion of the Ilısu Dam, in 2020.

ABOVE:

Confluence of Tigris and Euphrates Rivers, Iraq
The ancient region of Mesopotamia was centred on the fertile land between the Tigris and Euphrates Rivers. From around 8000 BCE, farmers began to settle in villages here. There is evidence that the earliest irrigation canals were dug from these rivers, in around 4000 BCE.

LEFT:

Tigris River, Baghdad, Iraq
Baghdad, founded in the eighth century and Iraq's capital, lies on the Tigris. During the city's 'golden age' in the ninth and 10th centuries, it was crisscrossed by canals, used for irrigation, drainage and transport. Today, water taxis ferry passengers along the river.

OPPOSITE:

Tigris River, central Iraq
For the Sumerians, the first literate people of Mesopotamia, the Tigris was filled by the god of water and creation, Enki, bringing life to their arid region. The ancient cities of Nineveh, Seleucia and Ctesiphon grew up on the river's banks.

Karun-4 Lake, Iran
The River Karun was dammed near Shahr-e-Kord in 2010. The numerous dams on the river generate hydroelectricity and provide flood control but have profoundly affected sediment transport. Some scholars identify the Karun as one of the four rivers of Eden, as described in Genesis 2:10–14, the others being the Tigris, Euphrates and possibly the Wadi Al-Batin.

Asia and Oceania

The Yangtze is the longest river in Asia, dwarfing Australia's 2508-km (1558-mile) Murray River, the greatest river of Oceania. The Yangtze flows for 6300km (3900 miles) from the Tibetan Plateau to the East China Sea. The river and its fertile valley have been central to China's development since the fifth millennium BCE. During the Han Dynasty (202 BCE–220 CE), irrigation systems and dykes were being constructed through the river valley, protecting this ever more important agricultural region from drought and flood. From 483 BCE, the Han Gou Canal linked the Yangtze with the Huai River. Over the centuries, the canal system, known as the Grand Canal, was extended to link Beijing with the Yangtze and Yellow Rivers. The canal and its far-reaching rivers spurred on China's economy and political integration. Today, the Yangtze's drainage basin is home to 400 million people. The Yangtze Delta is a megalopolis, boasting Shanghai, Nanjing and many other closely nestled cities. The delta is responsible for 20 per cent of China's gross domestic product. The world's largest hydroelectric power station, the Three Gorges Dam, was constructed on the Yangtze between 1994 and 2003. The dam supplies electricity to millions, but this emblem of the battle between economic progress and ecological damage has also profoundly affected the river's biodiversity and sediment transport.

OPPOSITE:

Indus River, Pakistan
From its source on the Tibetan Plateau, the Indus flows through India and Pakistan to the Arabian Sea. From around 3300 BCE, it was on the banks of the Indus that one of the world's earliest civilizations flourished. Cities such as Mohenjo-daro had complex sanitation systems, including private and public bathrooms and underground sewers.

Kabul River, Afghanistan
The Kabul flows eastward
through Afghanistan to meet
the Indus in Pakistan. In this
much-fought-over region,
the river has been the site of
numerous battles, including
a disaster during the Second
Anglo-Afghan War (1878–80),
described by Rudyard Kipling
in his '*Ford o' Kabul River*':
'Gawd 'elp 'em if they
blunder, for their boots'll
pull 'em under, By the ford o'
Kabul river in the dark.'

OPPOSITE BOTTOM:

**Shah-du-Shamshira Mosque,
Kabul, Kabul River,
Afghanistan**
The city of Kabul takes its
name from the river on which
it stands. The city grew up as
a centre for trade, thanks to
its location on the crossroads
between the north–south trail
through the Hindu Kush and
the east–west route along the
Kabul River.

LEFT:

**Kabul River, Kabul,
Afghanistan**
Since the start of the 21st
century, the Kabul has been
little more than a trickle here
for most of the year, in large
part due to damming and
climate change.

**Tarbela Dam,
Indus River, Pakistan**
The 1976 Tarbela Dam is the
world's largest earth-filled
dam, 143m (470ft) high and
2743m (9000ft) long. The dam
was made possible by the 1960
Indus Waters Treaty between
Pakistan and India, which
designated each country's
share of Indus Basin flow.

FAR RIGHT:
Indus River, Ladakh, India
The stretch of the Indus in
Ladakh is the only part of the
river in India. The word India
comes from the Indus, itself
named for the Sanskrit word
for river (*sindhu*). The term
'India' was originally just
applied to the lands on the
river's east bank, but by
300 BCE, Greek geographers
were using it to refer to the
whole subcontinent.

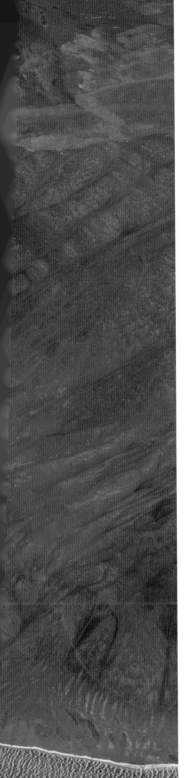

FAR LEFT AND LEFT TOP:

Indus River, Ladakh, India
The Indus and its tributaries, the Gilgit and Shyok, separate the Karakoram Range from the Himalayas. The river's cycle follows the seasons. In winter, the Indus freezes along its upper course, while its flow shrinks. During the July to September monsoon, the river frequently bursts its banks.

LEFT BOTTOM:

Indus River, Skardu Valley, Gilgit-Baltistan, Pakistan
Khardong Hill juts from the wide Skardu Valley, itself surrounded by the peaks of the Karakoram Range. While climate change is allowing the valley's farmers to grow a wider range of crops, reduced snowmelt is resulting in diminished water for irrigation in the Indus Basin, which covers 65 per cent of Pakistan.

ABOVE AND RIGHT:

Ganges River, Varanasi, India

Varanasi is the holiest of the Sapta Puri, the seven holy sites of Hinduism. The city is a place of pilgrimage for Hindus who believe that being cremated on the riverbank or having their ashes immersed in the Ganges will allow them to break the cycle of rebirth. On the city's 81 ghats, or riverfront steps, pilgrims perform ritual ablutions in the Ganges, the most sacred river and worshipped as Ganga, goddess of purification and forgiveness of sins.

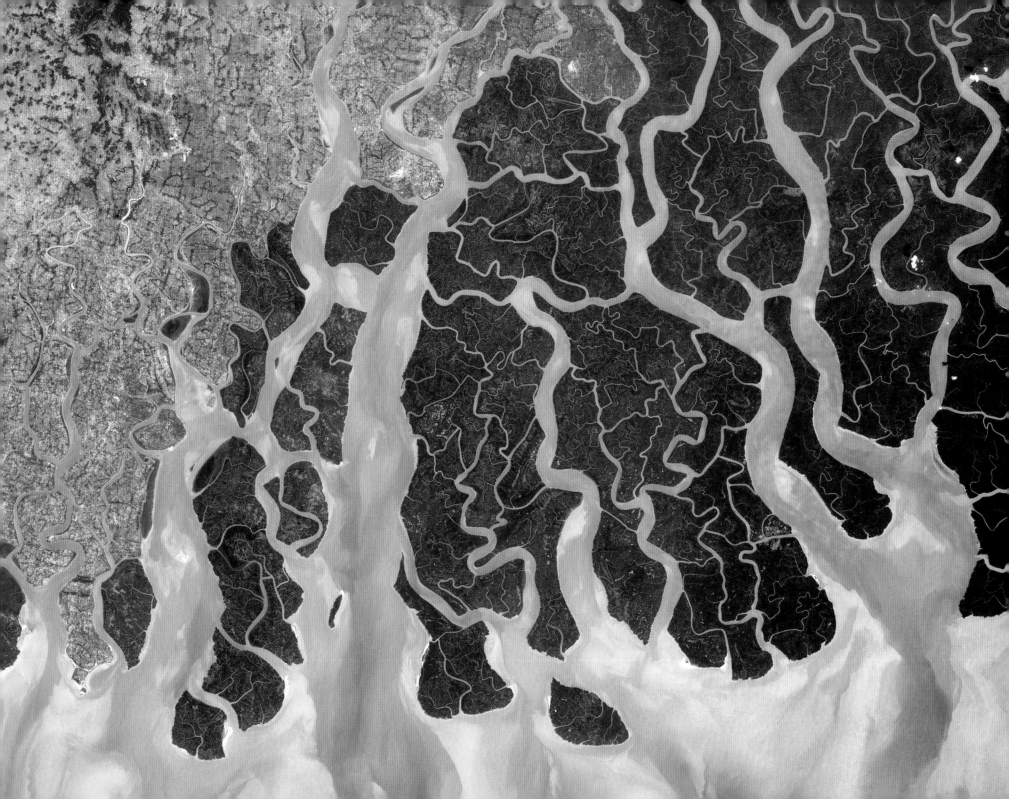

OPPOSITE:

Ganges Delta, India and Bangladesh

The world's largest river delta, covering 105,000 sq km (41,000 sq miles), the Ganges Delta carries the waters of the Ganges and Brahmaputra river systems into the Bay of Bengal. Despite the risks of flooding, 125 million people live in the delta, drawn by the fishing and the fertile soil on which they grow tea and rice.

ABOVE:

Pontoon Bridges, Allahabad, Ganges River, India

During the Kumbh Mela festival, held every 12 years, over 50 million Hindus visit the Triveni Sangam ('Meeting of Three Rivers'), the confluence of the Ganges, Yamuna and Saraswati rivers. Bathing here is believed to wash away all sins. The pontoon bridges float on metal tanks.

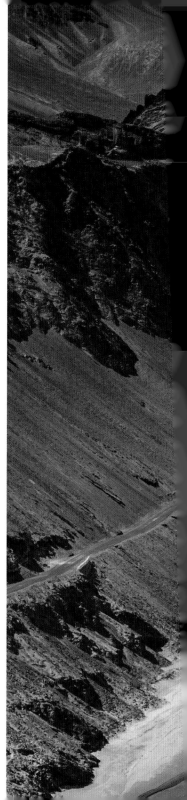

ABOVE:

Narmada River, Madhya Pradesh, India
The Narmada flows east to west across India, along a rift valley
between the Satpura and Vindhya ranges. For Hindus, the
Narmada is one of India's seven holy rivers. Smooth ellipsoid
stones found on the riverbed, called Banalinga, are said to take
the shape of the god Shiva's emblem, or lingam, and are used for
worship in temples and homes.

RIGHT:

Zanskar River, Ladakh, India
Between mid-January and mid-February, when the temperature
regularly falls to -35°C (-31°F), the Zanskar freezes over, making
its icy surface the only route from the village of Zanskar to the
city of Leh. Today, adventurous travellers from across the world
walk the route, known as the Chadar (or 'Thick Sheet of
Ice') Trek.

LEFT TOP:

Kelani River, Sri Lanka
The Kelani travels from the Sri Padma Mountains to the coast at Colombo, where it provides 80 per cent of the capital's drinking water. However, sand mining is deepening the river and causing saltwater intrusion. Up to 800,000 sq m (8.6 million sq ft) of sand is taken from the river annually, usually by divers with buckets.

LEFT BOTTOM:

Maha Oya River, Sri Lanka
Over one million people live along the banks of the 128km (80 mile) Maha Oya, relying on the watercourse for drinking water, irrigation and fishing.

RIGHT AND OPPOSITE (ALL):

Buriganga River, Dhaka, Bangladesh
In highly riverine Bangladesh, the Buriganga, which flows through the outskirts of Dhaka, is of vital importance for transport from taxis to tankers. The river is also one of the world's most polluted, receiving much of the city's sewage and household waste as well as untreated chemical waste from tanneries and factories.

Li River, Guilin, China
The Li runs through the karst landscapes of Guilin, where, over millions of years, peaks and caves have been worn away from the Triassic limestone. Towers form as vertical joints in the rock are eroded downward by acidic rainwater. The fertile, sediment-rich soil of the broad floodplain is ideal for growing rice.

LEFT:

Yangtze River, Yunnan Province, China
Intense river traffic, damming and plastic pollution are threatening many of the Yangtze's species, including the Yangtze sturgeon and narrow-ridged finless porpoise. The *baiji* may have been driven to extinction, making it the first dolphin species wiped out by human activities.

ABOVE:

Three Gorges, Yangtze River, China
Along the middle reaches of the Yangtze, among the Wu Mountains, are three adjacent gorges spanning over 300km (190 miles). In the fourth century, the official Yuan Shansong wrote of the gorges: 'I can raise up my head to appreciate what's above, and look down to see reflections, and the more acquainted I get with this place, the better I feel.'

Three Gorges Tribe Scenic Spot, Yangtze River, China
Just downstream from the Three Gorges Dam, at the
confluence of the Longjin Brook and Yangtze River,
traditional fishing villages of the Tujia people have been
preserved. The dam displaced 1.3 million local people and
flooded 1300 archaeological sites, although most were moved
to higher ground.

Nanjing Dashengguan, Yangtze River, China
Opened in 2005, this 1288m (4226ft) long expressway bridge spans the Yangtze in the industrial city of Nanjing. Until 1957, there were no bridges across the Yangtze from Yibin, in Sichuan, to the river's estuary at Shanghai. In that year, a road and rail bridge was completed at Wuhan, creating a much-needed transport link between northern and southern China.

OPPOSITE:
Yellow River, Shanxi, China
In Pianguan County, the Yellow River (Huang He) meets the Great Wall. On a cliff above the water is a 30m (98ft) watchtower. Legend has it that this bend in the Yellow River, known as Old Ox River Bend (Laoniuwan), formed when an ox was startled by a twinkling light, making it turn suddenly, ploughing a curving furrow that filled with water.

RIGHT:
Hukou Waterfall, Yellow River, China
The world's largest yellow waterfall thanks to the river's muddy sediments, Hukou has a height of 20m (66ft) and a width of 30 to 50m (98 to 164ft) depending on the season. The Hukou, which means 'flask mouth', formed where the wide river's flow is forced through a narrow opening between erosion-resistant rocks.

191

ABOVE:

**Yellow River,
Qinghai, China**
The Yellow River is named
for the yellow colour of its
water, the result of the river's
high sediment load. Much
of the sediment is picked up
on the Loess Plateau, which
covers 640,000 sq km (250,000
sq miles) of northern China.
From Qinghai the Yellow
River flows for 5464km (3395
miles) to the Bohai Sea.

RIGHT:

**First Bend of the Yellow
River, Sichuan, China**
Where the White River joins
the Yellow River, China's
second longest waterway
forms great S bends across
the Maqu Grassland.

LEFT TOP:

Yalu River Broken Bridge, China

The Yalu River forms a stretch of the border between China and North Korea. This truncated railway bridge between the Chinese city of Dandong and the Korean city of Sinuiju was bombed during the Korean War. The four remaining spans on the Chinese side are now a viewing platform.

LEFT BOTTOM:

Shinano River, Niigata City, Japan

At 367km (228 miles), the Shinano is the longest river in Japan, flowing from Honshu's Japanese Alps to the Sea of Japan. During the Sengoku period (1467–1615) of civil war, the Battle of Kawanakajima (1555) was fought here for control of the region.

RIGHT:

Chao Phraya River, Bangkok, Thailand

In Bangkok, the Chao Phraya is a highway for cargo ships, buses and taxis. During the Ayutthaya Kingdom (1350–1767), the meandering course of the river between Ayutthaya and the sea was shortened by a series of canals.

RIGHT AND FAR RIGHT:

Mekong River, Thailand
The Mekong courses for
4909km (3050 miles) from
the Tibetan Plateau to the
South China Sea, passing
through (or along the borders
between) China, Myanmar,
Laos, Thailand, Cambodia
and Vietnam. Biodiversity in
the Mekong is second only to
the Amazon, generating one
of the world's most productive
inland fisheries, with an
annual catch of two million
tonnes of fish.

LEFT:

**Khwae Yai
River Bridge, Thailand**
Bridge 277 of the Burma
Railway crosses the Khwae
Yai near Kanchanaburi. From
1940 to 1944 the Empire of
Japan used forced labour to
construct the railway, causing
the deaths of 12,000 Allied
prisoners of war and 90,000
Southeast Asian civilians.

RIGHT TOP:

Khwae Noi River, Thailand
The Khwae Noi merges with
the Khwae Yai to form the
Mae Klong. Until the 1960s,
the Khwae Yai was known as
part of the Mae Klong. In a
case of reality copying fiction,
it was renamed to match its
(entirely mistaken) name in
David Lean's 1957 movie, *The
Bridge on the River Kwai.*

RIGHT BOTTOM:

Irrawaddy River, Myanmar
The 2210km (1370 mile)
Irrawaddy has been an
important commercial
waterway since the sixth
century when the Bamars used
it to reap wealth from China
to India trade.

ABOVE AND RIGHT:

Mekong River, Cambodia

During the monsoon, the Mekong swells to a torrent, causing frequent flooding from Cambodia's Phnom Penh through the delta in Vietnam. Some of the floodwater surges into the Tonlé Sap River which then flows backwards, away from the sea. This phenomenon makes the Tonlé Sap the world's only seasonally reversing river.

**Si Phan Don,
Mekong River, Laos**
In the Mekong River
of southern Laos is the
archipelago of Si Phan Don
(meaning 'Four Thousand
Islands'). While some 'islands'
are nothing more than rocks
that are submerged during the
rainy season, the largest, Don
Det and Don Khon, are home
to farms, temples, schools
and hotels.

**Mekong Delta,
Near Châu Đọc, Vietnam**
More than half of Vietnam's
rice and fish comes from the
delta region. In addition to
agriculture and fishing, the
economy around Châu Đọc is
based on catfish farming, the
production of fermented fish
sauce (known here as *nuoc
mam*) and tourism.

**Golden Buddha, Pakse,
Mekong River, Laos**
A statue of the Buddha
watches over the city of Pakse
which lies at the confluence
of the Mekong and Xe Don
Rivers. Since 2000, the Lao
Nippon Bridge over the
Mekong, built with Japanese
support, has made Pakse a
centre for trade with Thailand
and beyond.

Mekong River, Laos
Laos is almost entirely within
the Mekong Basin. In this
mountainous, landlocked
country, the river has always
had immense economic
importance. Today, Laos is
focussing on becoming the
'battery of Asia' by selling
hydroelectricity made by
dozens of dams along the
river, its tributaries and the
nation's other rivers.

Tembeling River, Malaysia
The Tembeling runs through
the Taman Negara national
park in peninsular Malaysia.
The rainforest, dating back
130 million years, is home
to rare mammals such as
the Malayan tiger, guar and
Asian elephant.

OPPOSITE TOP:
Mersing River, Malaysia
Coursing from the forested
mountains of Johor state, the
Mersing's mouth lies on the
South China Sea at the ferry
port of Mersing. Along the
way, the river flows through
plantations of rubber, palm
oil and pineapples.

OPPOSITE BOTTOM:
Sarawak River, Malaysia
The stilted homes of
traditional Malay fishing
villages line the banks of
the Sarawak River, on the
island of Borneo. Fishermen
here must beware of the
occasionally aggressive
crocodiles that are in
competition for large, locally
prized fish such as *semah*
and *empurau*.

LEFT:

Martapura River, Kalimantan, Indonesia
The Lok Baintan floating market is said to have taken place for 500 years. The mainly female traders gather at sunrise in their *junkung* canoes, bartering produce from rambutans to guavas.

LEFT BOTTOM:

Ayung River, Bali, Indonesia
The longest river on the island of Bali, the 68km (42 mile) Ayung flows through rice terraces to the Badung Strait. The Ayung's rapids make it popular with rafters.

RIGHT:

Western New Guinea, Indonesia
On New Guinea, 70,000 Asmat people live among the rivers of the lowland rainforest. Woodcarvers are highly valued as they produce both canoes and stilted homes.

LEFT:

Billabong Near Wilcannia, Darling River, Australia

'Billabong' is the Australian term for an oxbow lake, a pond left behind when a river changes course. In desert and semi-arid regions, billabongs had great significance to Aboriginal Australians and European explorers and farmers. Billabongs find their way into the work of landscape painters such as Tjyllyungoo as well as the bush ballad 'Waltzing Matilda'.

BELOW:

Kallang Basin, Singapore

The Kallang Basin receives the waters of the Kallang, Geylang and Rochor Rivers. In the background is the luxury hotel Marina Bay Sands. Designed by Moshe Safdie, it consists of three towers linked by the 340m (1120ft) long SkyPark. In 2014, only two wild otters were spotted in the Kallang River in Singapore's Bishan Park, but the population is growing.

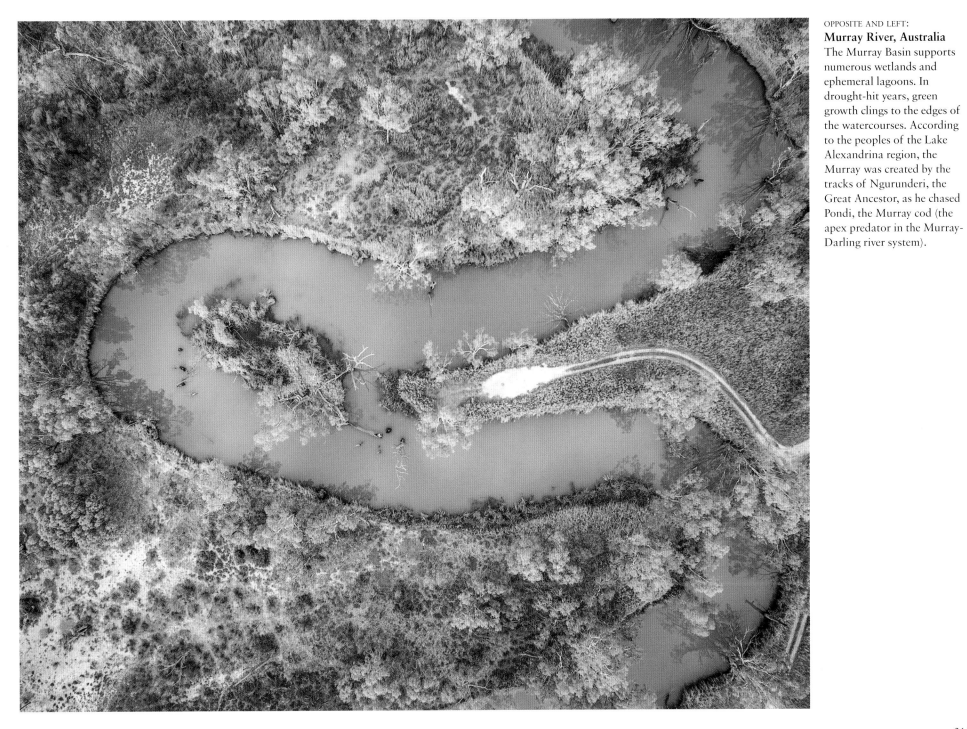

Murray River, Australia
The Murray Basin supports numerous wetlands and ephemeral lagoons. In drought-hit years, green growth clings to the edges of the watercourses. According to the peoples of the Lake Alexandrina region, the Murray was created by the tracks of Ngurunderi, the Great Ancestor, as he chased Pondi, the Murray cod (the apex predator in the Murray-Darling river system).

215

Yarra River, Melbourne, Australia

Since Melbourne was founded at the mouth of the Yarra River in 1835, the river's lower course has been transformed. To protect the city against flood, the river has been widening and dams such as the Upper Yarra Reservoir constructed.

RIGHT:
Westport, Buller Estuary, New Zealand
The waters of the Buller travel 170km (110 miles) across South Island, from Lake Rotoiti to the Tasman Sea at the port of Westport. Maori had lived along the west coast since the early 14th century, but Westport became the first European settlement there when a group of gold miners arrived in 1861.

OPPOSITE TOP AND BOTTOM:
Buller River, New Zealand
The Buller River was named after the British MP Charles Buller, director of the New Zealand Company, which financed English colonization of New Zealand between 1825 and 1858. The Maori name for the Buller is *Kawatiri*, meaning 'deep and swift'.

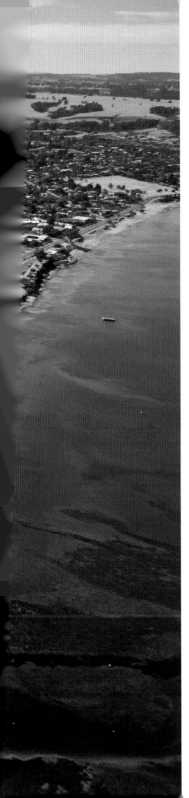

OPPOSITE:

Taupo, Waikato River, New Zealand

From Lake Taupo (*pictured*), New Zealand's largest lake, the Waikato runs northwestward for 425km (264 miles). In 1863, Maori living between Auckland and the Waikato were told to pledge allegiance to Queen Victoria or be expelled south of the river. Today, the Tanui are pursuing their legal rights to the river.

LEFT:

Huka Falls, Waikato River, New Zealand

This series of small waterfalls, the tallest 11m (36ft) high, formed where New Zealand's longest river narrows abruptly to flow through a granite canyon. *Huka* means 'foam' in Maori, a fitting name for water that surges at a rate of 220 cu m (7770 cu ft) per second.

LEFT AND ABOVE:
Mataura River, New Zealand
The Mataura flows through Southland, passing under the
bridges at Gore (*above*) before meeting the Pacific Ocean
at Toetoes Bay. The first bridge at Gore was a rail bridge,
constructed in 1875. It was not until 1890 when the ford across
the river had claimed many casualties, that the town gained a
road bridge. Much of the Mataura's course is braided, with
sediment deposits forming small, sometimes temporary, islands.

Picture Credits